100 facts

Extreme Survival

100 facts

Extreme Survival

Jen Green

Consultant: Andrew Price

Miles Kelly

First published in 2010 by Miles Kelly Publishing Ltd
Harding's Barn, Bardfield End Green, Thaxted, Essex, CM6 3PX, UK

2 4 6 8 10 9 7 5 3

EDITORIAL DIRECTOR Belinda Gallagher
ART DIRECTOR Jo Brewer
EDITOR Carly Blake
VOLUME DESIGNERS Jo Brewer, Andrea Slane
IMAGE MANAGER Liberty Newton
INDEXER Gill Lee
PRODUCTION MANAGER Elizabeth Collins
REPROGRAPHICS Anthony Cambray, Stephan Davis, Ian Paulyn

ISBN 978-1-84810-307-8

Printed in China

British Library Cataloguing-in-Publication Data
A catalogue record for this book is available from the British Library

ACKNOWLEDGEMENTS

The publishers would like to thank the following artists who have contributed to this book:
Kayleigh Allen, Julian Baker, Mike Foster, Andrea Morandi, Nick Spender
All other artwork from the Miles Kelly Artwork Bank

The publishers would like to thank the following sources for the use of their photographs:
t = top, b = bottom, l = left, r = right, c = centre
Cover Sipa Press/Rex Features
Page 2–3 Stephen Alvarez/National Geographic Stock, 6–7 Andrew Querner/Getty Images; 8 Pedre/iStockphoto.com; 9(t) Forgiss/Fotolia.com,
(b) Ed Kosmicki/AFP/Getty Images; 11(t) Mtomczak/Dreamstime.com, (b) Andrew Price; 12 Andrew Price; 13 Blickwinkel/Alamy; 14(t) Annie
Griffiths Belt/Getty Images, (b) Alex Hibbert/Photolibrary; 15(t) Time & Life Pictures/Getty Images, (b) Ashely Cooper/SpecialistStock/
SplashdownDirect/Rex Features; 16 Articophoto/Alamy; 17 Yvette Cardozo/Photolibrary; 20 Kapu/Fotolia.com; 21(c) AFP/Gety Images,
(b) Sipa Press/Rex Features; 24–25 Michael Freeman/Corbis; 24 Taylor S. Kennedy/Getty Images; 26(b) 2001 Credit: Topham Picturepoint
Topfoto.co.uk; 27 Bill Bachman/Alamy; 28(t) Mark Hannaford/Photolibrary, mosquito Vladvitek/Dreamstime.com, (br) Mark Moffett/Minden
Pictures/National Geographic Stock; 29 National Geographic/Getty Images; 30(c) Roberto Caputo/Getty Images, (b) Robin Hanbury-
Tenison/Photolibrary; 31 Time and Life Pictures/Getty Images; 36–37 Keith Brooks/Fotolia.com; 37(t) Moviestore Collection Ltd; 40(bl) Holger
Mette/Fotolia.com, (br) Dadang Tri/Reuters/Corbis; 41 Roger Ressmeyer/Corbis; 42 Carsten Peter/Getty Images; 43(t) Bloomberg via Getty
Images, (b) alohaspirit/iStockphoto.com; 42–43 AFP/Getty Images; 45(t) S Robertson/Newspix/Rex Features, (c) c.MGM/Everett/Rex Features;
46(b) jeffix/iStockphoto.com; 47 Geoff Moore/Rex Features

All other photographs are from:
Corel, digitalSTOCK, digitalvision, Dreamstime.com, Fotolia.com, iStockphoto.com,
John Foxx, PhotoAlto, PhotoDisc, PhotoEssentials, PhotoPro, Stockbyte

Every effort has been made to acknowledge the source and copyright holder of each picture.
Miles Kelly Publishing apologises for any unintentional errors or omissions.

Made with paper from a sustainable forest

www.mileskelly.net   info@mileskelly.net

www.factsforprojects.com

The publishers would like
to thank *Bushcraft &
Survival Skills Magazine*
for their help in
compiling this book.

BUSHCRAFT
& SURVIVAL SKILLS
magazine
www.bushcraftmagazine.com

Self-publish your
children's book

buddingpress.co.uk

Contents

Surviving extremes

1 **Extreme survival means staying alive in a dangerous situation, and preparation is often the key.** In the most perilous places, knowing how to find food and water, build a shelter and light a fire can mean the difference between life and death. Survival experts test themselves by spending time in the wild. Peoples such as the Inuit of the Arctic use traditional skills to survive. Other people find themselves in danger unexpectedly. But even in an emergency there are things you can do to stay alive.

▲ In extreme situations, such as climbing a sheer-sided ice pillar, the body's own survival mechanisms are activated, which help you to stay alive.

2 **Water is your body's greatest need.** You can survive for three weeks without food, but only a few days without water. You need to drink two to three litres of water a day to replace the moisture you lose as you sweat, breathe and urinate.

▼ A balanced diet includes four main food groups: Carbohydrates, protein, fibre and fats. A healthy diet helps prepare the body for extreme survival.

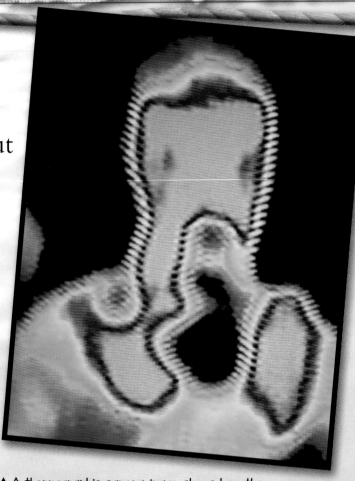

▲ A thermographic camera image shows how the body gives off heat. Uncovered areas, such as the face (shown in white) lose heat the fastest.

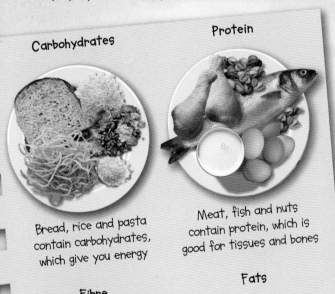

Carbohydrates

Protein

Bread, rice and pasta contain carbohydrates, which give you energy

Meat, fish and nuts contain protein, which is good for tissues and bones

Fibre

Fats

Fresh vegetables and fruit provide fibre, which aids digestion

Foods such as cheese and oil contain fats, which provide energy and are good for general health

3 **The human body maintains a temperature of 37°C.** In extreme cold, you are at risk of hypothermia. If you feel cold and start to shiver, put on more clothes or get to a warm place. In extreme heat you may overheat, and feel sick and dizzy. Rest in the shade and drink water.

4 **Food is the fuel your body needs to stay warm and active.** You need to eat a variety of different foods to stay healthy, including protein such as meat or fish, and carbohydrates such as bread, rice or cereal. You also need fibre, fats, sugars and salt.

5 **Keeping fit will improve your chances of survival.** Train for an expedition by taking energetic exercise at least three times a week, such as swimming, jogging and playing sports. Getting used to an environment can also help you survive. Some polar explorers take icy baths to get used to extreme cold!

◄ Cycling improves fitness and stamina, so you can keep going for longer. It also strengthens muscles.

6 **American climber Aron Ralston's will to survive saved his life.** Aron was climbing in a canyon in Utah, USA, in 2003, when his hand got trapped under a boulder. After six days, still unable to free himself, he realized no one was coming to look for him. To save his life, Aron cut off his own hand using a multi-tool knife and staggered to safety.

► Aron had to break the bones in his lower arm before he could cut off his hand.

I DON'T BELIEVE IT!

People who are very hungry have eaten raw cockroaches, maggots, lizards and scorpions. In times of starvation rats, cats and dogs have all been made into stews.

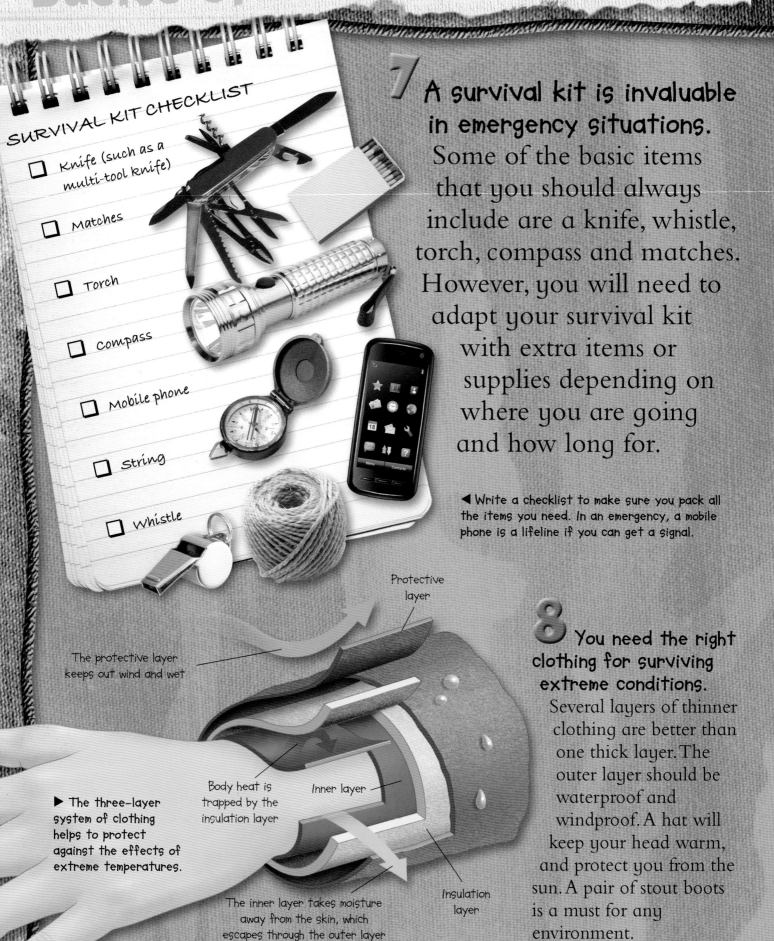

SURVIVAL KIT CHECKLIST

- ☐ Knife (such as a multi-tool knife)
- ☐ Matches
- ☐ Torch
- ☐ Compass
- ☐ Mobile phone
- ☐ String
- ☐ Whistle

7 **A survival kit is invaluable in emergency situations.** Some of the basic items that you should always include are a knife, whistle, torch, compass and matches. However, you will need to adapt your survival kit with extra items or supplies depending on where you are going and how long for.

◀ Write a checklist to make sure you pack all the items you need. In an emergency, a mobile phone is a lifeline if you can get a signal.

Protective layer

The protective layer keeps out wind and wet

▶ The three-layer system of clothing helps to protect against the effects of extreme temperatures.

Body heat is trapped by the insulation layer

Inner layer

The inner layer takes moisture away from the skin, which escapes through the outer layer

Insulation layer

8 **You need the right clothing for surviving extreme conditions.** Several layers of thinner clothing are better than one thick layer. The outer layer should be waterproof and windproof. A hat will keep your head warm, and protect you from the sun. A pair of stout boots is a must for any environment.

9 A first aid kit is vital to treat injury and illness quickly. Your kit should include antiseptic wipes to clean wounds, bandages, plasters, and painkillers such as aspirin. It's a good idea to take sun lotion and insect repellent, too.

KEY

① Plasters

② Microporous tape

③ Scissors

④ Painkillers

⑤ Bandage

▶ Check your first aid kit before you set off anywhere to make sure it is well stocked.

10 Keep a cool head in an emergency. First, get yourself out of immediate danger and treat any injuries you may have. Then assess the situation — are you likely to be rescued soon? If not, how will you secure the basics — water, food and shelter?

11 Finding water is a priority. Valley bottoms and cracks in rocks are good places to look. When possible collect rain water. In cold environments you can melt snow. If you don't have purifying tablets, boil water for 15 minutes to make it safe to drink.

MAKE A BASIC SHELTER

You will need:
one long stick (longer than your body)
two shorter sticks (70 cm long)
string, rope or twine   plastic sheet

1. Bind the two shorter sticks together near their ends to make a cross, and stand them up.
2. Bind the long stick to them where they cross to form the sloping roof.
3. Drape the plastic sheet over the stick frame to form the shelter. Weight the edges of the plastic with stones.

▼ Fill your bottle from a flowing stream rather than still water.

Staying alive

12 If you are spending a few days in the wild you will need a proper camp. Site your camp in a sheltered place and choose a patch of clear, flat ground. Be careful not to set up too near a river as it could flood after rain.

13 A fire provides warmth and heat for cooking. It also gives you a mental boost and could attract rescue. Prepare your materials: Dry grass or straw for tinder, small sticks for kindling and larger sticks for fuel. Use matches, a fire steel, or a knife and flint to light your fire.

▼ A fire steel produces sparks to ignite dry tinder such as straw or grass. Striking a knife against a flint will also make a spark.

Ensure there are no overhead dangers such as falling rocks or dead branches

▶ The location of your camp should have water and shelter. If you don't have a tent, build a makeshift shelter using branches or rocks.

If you are waiting for rescue, camp in a clearing where rescuers will be more likely to spot you

I DON'T BELIEVE IT!

Don't take too much kit! In 1860, Burke and Wills led an expedition across Australia. They took 20 tonnes of kit loaded on six wagons. It made them so slow that all their supplies ran out, and only one man returned alive.

Camp near a source of fresh water, but not too close as you may get bitten by insects

► With this method of fishing you can leave the line and return later. Attach baited hooks to a long line, weighted at one end, and secure the other end on the bank.

Bait

Weight

Hook

Try to find a location naturally sheltered from the wind

Position your fire well away from your tent

14 Finding food in the wild is a challenge. If you have a hook and line you could try fishing. For bait, use scraps of food or live worms. Small game could be snared using a noose made of string or wire set in places where animals are active.

15 If you are lost, don't panic. You can use the Sun to work out your direction. It rises in the east, shines in the south at midday, and sets in the west. At night, groups of stars show the way. You could climb a hill or tree to try to spot landmarks.

► The leaves of the North American compass plant always point north-south.

16 Wild foods such as nuts, berries and mushrooms can sometimes be eaten. However many plants and mushrooms are highly poisonous. You should never eat anything unless you can positively identify it.

17

With temperatures as low as −80°C, the polar regions are the coldest places on Earth. The Arctic in the north is an ice-covered ocean. Antarctica in the south is a huge landmass covered by ice 2–4 kilometres thick.

▶ The first sign of frostbite is waxy skin. Badly frostbitten flesh turns black and blistered.

Covering to prevent frostbite

Sunglasses

Safety ropes

Windproof and waterproof clothing

Gloves

Ski poles

◀ In very cold temperatures all of the skin should be covered to protect against frostbite.

Insulated boots

Skis

18

Hypothermia and frostbite are dangers in polar lands. Exposure to extreme cold can lead to frostbite – a condition where your skin and flesh freezes. Fingers, toes and noses are most at risk, so keep them covered. Hypothermia is a condition where your body temperature drops below 35°C, and can set in if you are cold and wet.

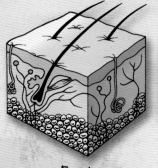

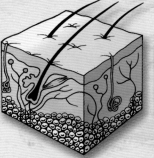

Frostnip
The surface layer of skin freezes, causing itchiness and pain. No lasting damage.

Superficial frostbite
The skin blisters and freezes but deep tissues are not affected.

Deep frostbite
Tissues, nerves and blood vessels below the skin are affected, causing numbness.

I DON'T BELIEVE IT!

British explorer Ranulph Fiennes suffered badly frostbitten fingers in the Arctic. When he returned home, he cut them off in his garden shed using an electric saw!

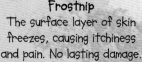

19 In 1910, two teams of explorers raced to be the first people to reach the South Pole. With husky dogs pulling their sledges, the Norwegian team was first to arrive, and returned home safely. The British hauled their own sledges and got to the pole 33 days later. Sadly, on their way back, the team died of cold and starvation.

▶ Mawson peers into the crevasse where his friend fell to his death when a fragile ice bridge gave way.

▼ Even for the emergency services, rescuing someone who has fallen through ice into freezing water is a difficult operation.

20 In 1912, Australian explorer Douglas Mawson was stranded on Antarctica. While crossing a glacier, his companion was killed when he fell into a crevasse, along with a sledge of supplies. Mawson struggled back to base camp only to see his ship sailing off! Luckily a few men had stayed behind to search for him, but it was a year before their ship could return.

21 Explorers take care to avoid thin ice. Just a few minutes in icy water can kill you. If you fall through the ice, turn around and try to climb out the way you came. Kick your legs and use a knife or keys to grip the ice to help you haul yourself out.

HYPOTHERMIA

Symptoms:
Uncontrollable shivering
Loss of coordination
Pale, cold skin
Headache
Blurred vision

Action:
Take shelter
Change out of wet clothing
Drink warm liquids

Menu

15

The Inuit of the Arctic

22 **The Inuit are the most northerly people on Earth.** For thousands of years they have lived in the Arctic regions of North America, and Greenland. This hardy people live traditionally by hunting animals such as seals and whales for meat, and skins to make clothes.

▲ An Inuit hunter in his kayak. He launches his harpoon using a throwing stick which makes the weapon go further.

23 **The Inuit diet is mostly meat, especially from seals.** Their word for seal means 'giver of life'. The Inuit hunt seals by crawling towards them across the ice, hiding behind white screens made of animal skin. Once within range, they kill their prey using a spear or gun. In summer the Inuit also gather birds' eggs and berries to eat.

QUIZ

1. The Inuit word for what animal means 'giver of life'?
2. What is a kayak?
3. What is the Inuit word for a hooded jacket?

Answers:
1. Seal 2. A one-man canoe 3. Anorak

24 **The Inuit travel over the ice on sledges pulled by husky dogs.** After a long day's hauling, the dogs will nestle down and sleep in the snow. When hunting at sea, the Inuit use one-man canoes called kayaks, which are powered with a two-ended paddle. The kayak is made of sealskin stretched over a wooden frame.

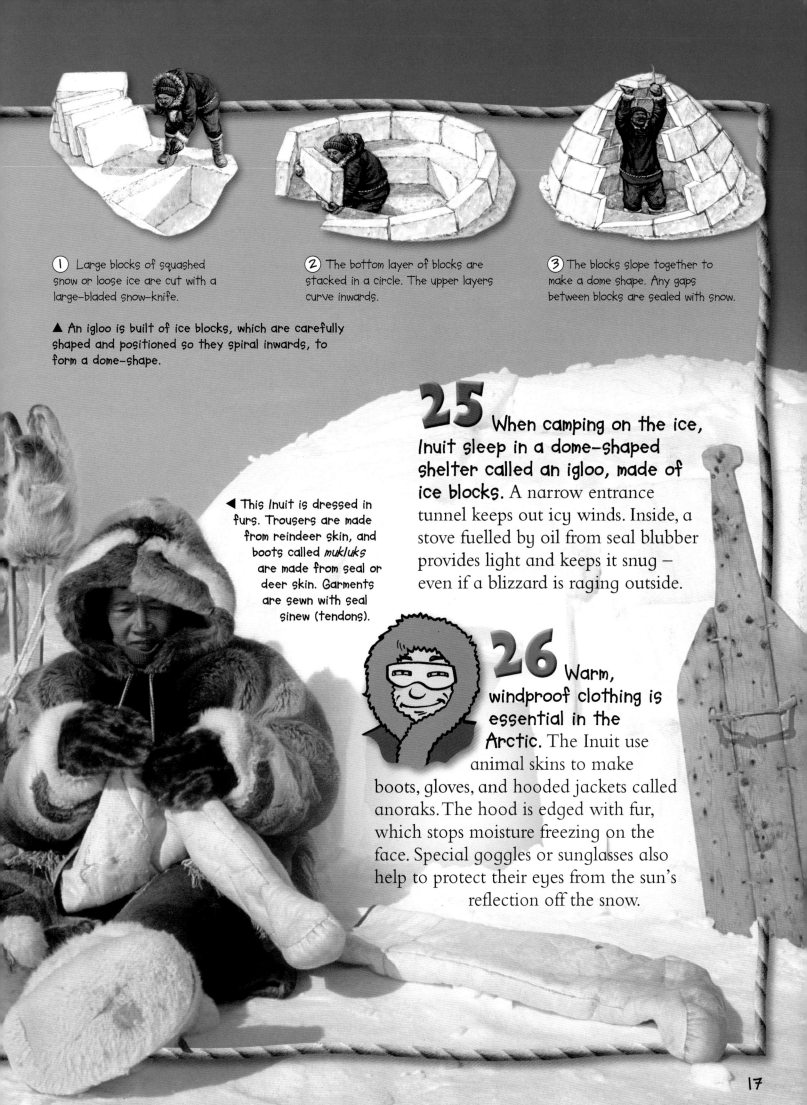

① Large blocks of squashed snow or loose ice are cut with a large-bladed snow-knife.

② The bottom layer of blocks are stacked in a circle. The upper layers curve inwards.

③ The blocks slope together to make a dome shape. Any gaps between blocks are sealed with snow.

▲ An igloo is built of ice blocks, which are carefully shaped and positioned so they spiral inwards, to form a dome-shape.

◄ This Inuit is dressed in furs. Trousers are made from reindeer skin, and boots called *mukluks* are made from seal or deer skin. Garments are sewn with seal sinew (tendons).

25 When camping on the ice, Inuit sleep in a dome-shaped shelter called an igloo, made of ice blocks. A narrow entrance tunnel keeps out icy winds. Inside, a stove fuelled by oil from seal blubber provides light and keeps it snug – even if a blizzard is raging outside.

26 Warm, windproof clothing is essential in the Arctic. The Inuit use animal skins to make boots, gloves, and hooded jackets called anoraks. The hood is edged with fur, which stops moisture freezing on the face. Special goggles or sunglasses also help to protect their eyes from the sun's reflection off the snow.

27 In 1914, Irish explorer Ernest Shackleton set out to cross Antarctica. His ship *Endurance* sailed from the island of South Georgia, but became trapped in sea ice. For nine months the ship drifted in the ice, before it began to sink. The 29 men and three lifeboats were stranded.

28 Shackleton decided to make for Antarctica across the ice, with the lifeboats. But they made slow progress. So the crew set up a camp and waited for the drifting ice to carry them to open water. After four months, they were at the water's edge.

▼ Shackleton's men tried to haul the heavy lifeboats, but it took them a week to cover just 11 kilometres.

I DON'T BELIEVE IT!

On Elephant Island Shackleton's crew survived on penguin meat and a stew of seaweed and shellfish. Occasionally they caught a seal and the fish in its stomach made a welcome change from the horrible stew!

29 In April, 1916, the men set off in the lifeboats for the nearest land – Elephant Island. Leaping killer whales threatened to capsize the boats, and the men had to bail out water constantly to avoid sinking. After a week they reached the island safely. It was 16 months since they had stood on land.

▶ The lifeboats were menaced by icebergs, towering waves and killer whales on the voyage to Elephant Island.

30 On Elephant Island there was no hope of rescue. The nearest inhabited land was a whaling station on South Georgia, 1100 kilometres away. With five men, Shackleton set sail again, battling stormy seas for 17 days to reach the island. Then Shackleton headed inland across mountains, towards the whaling station.

31 The men left on Elephant Island sheltered under upturned lifeboats. After four months on the island they spotted a ship in the distance. Shackleton had reached the whaling station and after several attempts, finally returned on a ship to rescue his crew.

▶ The crew marooned on bleak, windswept Elephant Island were overjoyed to be rescued after four months.

Mountain survival

32 High mountains are found on every continent. Thousands of people have climbed Mount Everest, the world's highest peak, but many have failed. Above 8000 metres is known as the 'Death Zone' because there is so little oxygen in the air. This can cause altitude sickness.

◄ Air with low oxygen doesn't hold the Sun's heat well. For every 150 metres of height gained, the temperature drops by 1°C.

33 Mountain explorers have to prepare for all weather, including extreme cold, hail, snow and storms. There is no shelter on a mountain so warm clothing is essential. Mountaineers use equipment such as ice axes to climb icy slopes, and metal spikes called crampons, which fix to their boots for extra grip. Climbers descend a mountain by abseiling (lowering on a rope).

34 Glaciers are rivers of ice that flow down from mountains and over land. Deep cracks called crevasses can be hidden by snow, making glaciers extremely dangerous to travel over. When crossing a glacier, climbers rope together for safety. If one climber falls in, another can haul him out.

Mount Everest (8850 metres)

8000 metres (Death Zone)

7000 metres

6000 metres

5000 metres

4000 metres

3000 metres

Altitude sickness can occur at 2400 metres and above

2000 metres

1000 metres

Sea level (0 metres)

Warm hat

Warm clothing

Sunglasses

Snowshoes

Ski poles

Waterproof boots

▲ Warm, waterproof clothing and safety equipment is vital. Snowshoes are useful for trekking across soft snow.

▶ Dogs are sometimes used by mountain rescue teams to sniff out people buried by avalanches.

ALTITUDE SICKNESS

Symptoms:
Nausea and vomiting
Dizziness
Shortness of breath

Action:
Rest
Drink water
Descend to a lower altitude

Menu   Contacts

35 An avalanche happens when a mass of snow and rock slides down a mountain. Avalanches can be triggered by heavy snowfall, melting snow or even a loud noise. If you are caught in one, use a swimming movement to stay near the surface.

▲ This sketch by Dutchman Sam van Haaster shows how he survived an avalanche by digging a snow cave.

36 In 1972, a plane carrying a rugby team crashed in the Andes Mountains. Many of the 45 passengers died in the crash or soon after. For the survivors, food soon ran out and they had no choice but to eat the flesh from their dead companions. After two months, two of the men trekked through mountains for 12 days to reach help.

▼ Survivors wave to rescuers. The crash site was so remote that aircraft could not spot the wreck.

Trapped in a crevasse

37 In 1985, British climber Joe Simpson narrowly escaped death while climbing in the Andes Mountains. With his friend Simon Yates, he had reached the summit of a sheer peak called Siula Grande. During their descent of the mountain the next day, joined together by a rope, Joe slipped and fell. The rope stopped his fall, but his knee hit a rock and shattered.

38 With a broken leg, Joe's position was desperate. Simon anchored himself in the snow and lowered Joe on the rope. Bit by bit, the pair descended 900 metres. But at dusk, Joe dropped off an overhanging cliff while being lowered. He plunged downwards and was left dangling in the air.

39 Joe was too heavy for Simon to haul back up again. His weight threatened to pull Simon off the cliff too, so Simon had no choice but to cut the rope. Joe dropped like a stone onto the glacier below and into a crevasse. Simon peered over and was convinced his friend was dead. He made his way back to camp alone.

◄ Dangling on the end of the rope with a badly broken leg, Joe's life hung in the balance.

40 **Joe had survived the 30-metre fall and landed on a narrow ledge partway down the crevasse.** Its walls were too sheer for him to climb out, so he pulled down the rest of the rope, secured the end and lowered himself deeper into the crevasse. His feet finally touched a fragile snow bridge, which he crawled across and up to the surface.

▶ A steep slope led up from the ice bridge in the crevasse to the surface. After reaching the surface, Joe collapsed.

41 **With determination, Joe began to crawl down the glacier towards camp.** With one leg useless, every move was agony. After three days of crawling he reached camp just before Simon was leaving. A mule carried Joe to safety. Against all the odds he had survived.

▶ It took Simon and Joe two days to reach the nearest civilization.

Deadly deserts

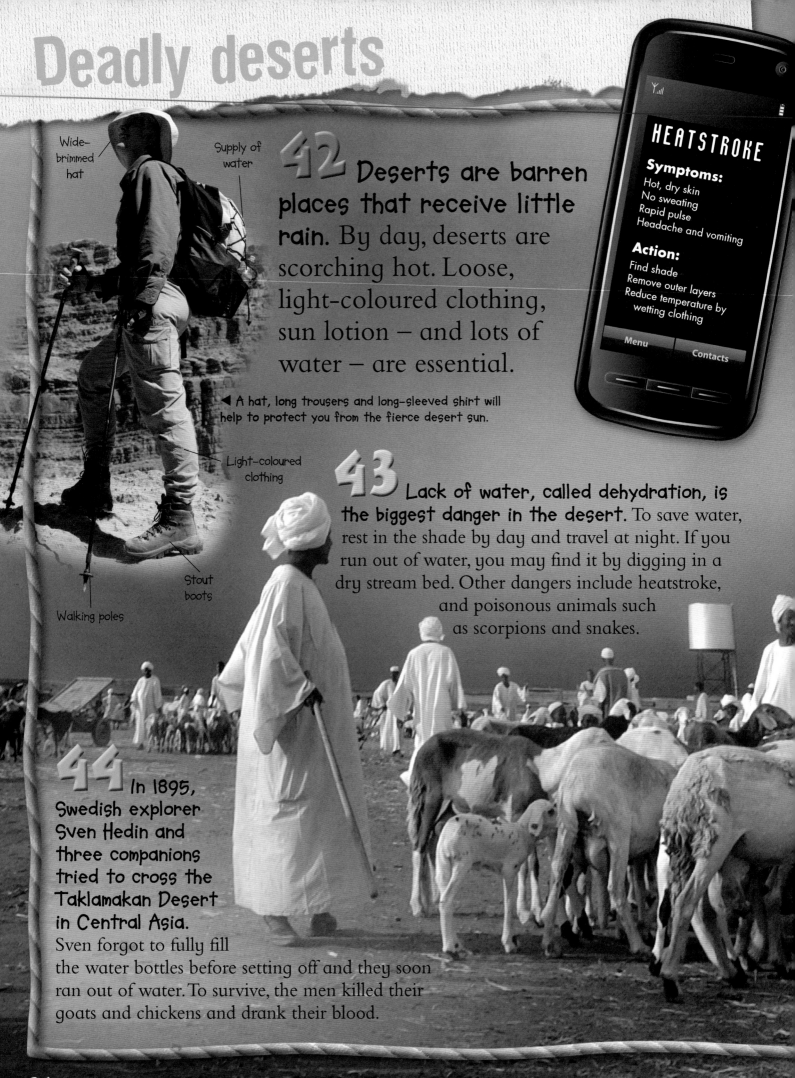

Wide-brimmed hat

Supply of water

Light-coloured clothing

Stout boots

Walking poles

42 Deserts are barren places that receive little rain. By day, deserts are scorching hot. Loose, light-coloured clothing, sun lotion – and lots of water – are essential.

◄ A hat, long trousers and long-sleeved shirt will help to protect you from the fierce desert sun.

43 Lack of water, called dehydration, is the biggest danger in the desert. To save water, rest in the shade by day and travel at night. If you run out of water, you may find it by digging in a dry stream bed. Other dangers include heatstroke, and poisonous animals such as scorpions and snakes.

44 In 1895, Swedish explorer Sven Hedin and three companions tried to cross the Taklamakan Desert in Central Asia. Sven forgot to fully fill the water bottles before setting off and they soon ran out of water. To survive, the men killed their goats and chickens and drank their blood.

HEATSTROKE

Symptoms:
Hot, dry skin
No sweating
Rapid pulse
Headache and vomiting

Action:
Find shade
Remove outer layers
Reduce temperature by wetting clothing

Menu   Contacts

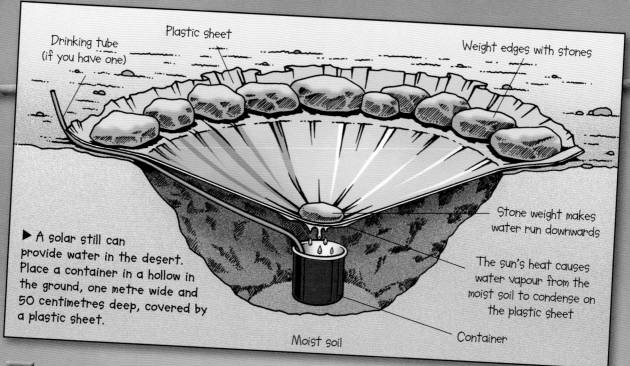

Drinking tube
(if you have one)

Plastic sheet

Weight edges with stones

Stone weight makes
water run downwards

The sun's heat causes
water vapour from the
moist soil to condense on
the plastic sheet

Container

Moist soil

▶ A solar still can provide water in the desert. Place a container in a hollow in the ground, one metre wide and 50 centimetres deep, covered by a plastic sheet.

45 Stinging sand fills the air when the wind whips up a sandstorm. If you see a dark cloud of sand approaching, find shelter quickly. The flying sand makes it hard to breathe, so cover your nose and mouth with a damp cloth, and protect your eyes.

46 In 1994, Italian marathon runner Mauro Prosperi got lost in the Sahara desert during a sandstorm. After 36 hours his food and water ran out. He survived by drinking his own urine and eating bats and snakes. After nine days lost in the desert, he was found by wandering nomads.

▲ Herdsmen watch as a sandstorm, known locally as a haboob, approaches a livestock market in East Africa.

DESERT HEADGEAR

This headgear will keep you cool and protect you from the burning desert sun.

You will need:
piece of thin rope   hankerchief
large cloth (approximately 120 cm square)

1. Fold the hankerchief into a wad and place it on the top of your head.
2. Drape the large cloth on top so that it covers your head and the back of your neck.
3. Tie the rope around your head to secure the cloth.

Desert wanderers

47 Aboriginal Australians are at home in the deserts of Australia, called the Outback. This ancient people have lived in the Outback for 50,000 years. They traditionally live a nomadic life, wandering from place to place. Women gather wild foods such as roots and berries, and men hunt animals for meat.

Kangaroo   Emu   Possum

▲ Aboriginals are familiar with the tracks of emus, kangaroos and possums, which they hunt for food.

48 Aboriginals are skilled at tracking. They can identify many different animals from their smeared prints in the dust. They can tell if the animal was injured and how fast it was moving. Hunters use spears, bows and arrows, or curved sticks called boomerangs to kill their prey.

▲ Spears are used to hunt fish and other water life, as well as larger prey such as kangaroos.

I DON'T BELIEVE IT!

Aboriginals sometimes drink from water-holding frogs. They dig up the plump frogs, which burrow underground, and squeeze them to drink the water. They let the frogs go again — thinner, but unharmed!

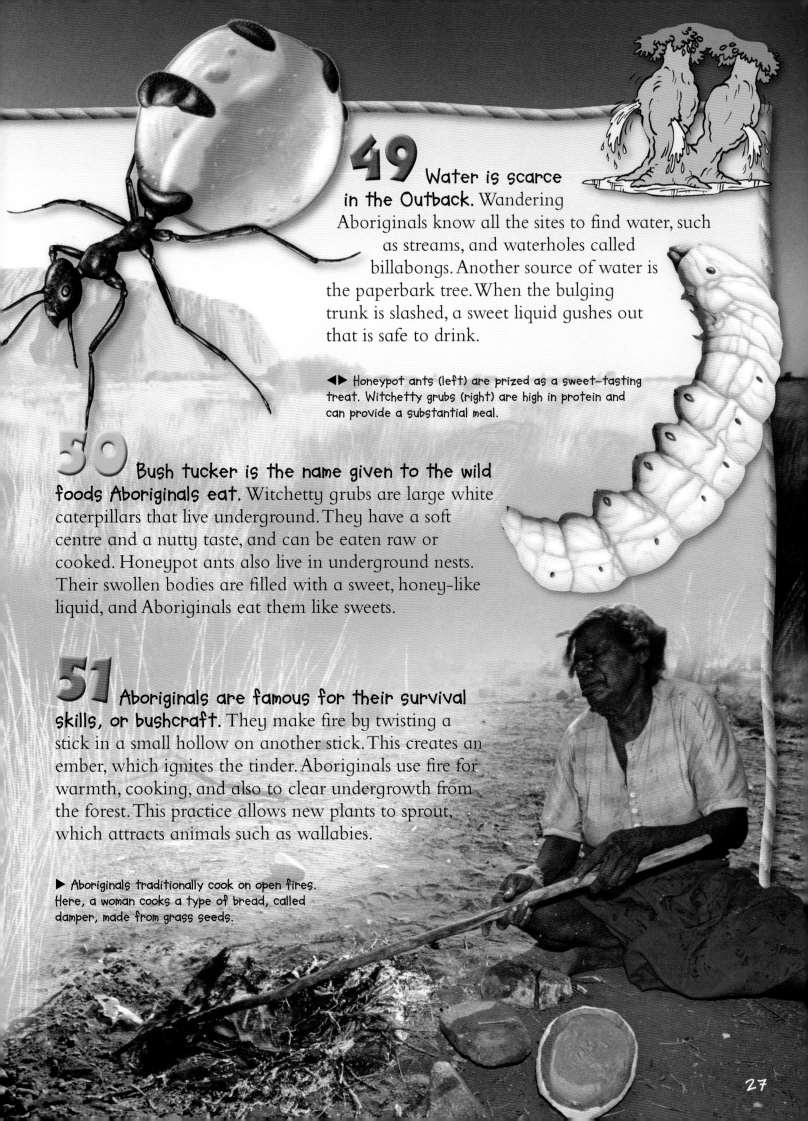

49 **Water is scarce in the Outback.** Wandering Aboriginals know all the sites to find water, such as streams, and waterholes called billabongs. Another source of water is the paperbark tree. When the bulging trunk is slashed, a sweet liquid gushes out that is safe to drink.

◄► Honeypot ants (left) are prized as a sweet-tasting treat. Witchetty grubs (right) are high in protein and can provide a substantial meal.

50 **Bush tucker is the name given to the wild foods Aboriginals eat.** Witchetty grubs are large white caterpillars that live underground. They have a soft centre and a nutty taste, and can be eaten raw or cooked. Honeypot ants also live in underground nests. Their swollen bodies are filled with a sweet, honey-like liquid, and Aboriginals eat them like sweets.

51 **Aboriginals are famous for their survival skills, or bushcraft.** They make fire by twisting a stick in a small hollow on another stick. This creates an ember, which ignites the tinder. Aboriginals use fire for warmth, cooking, and also to clear undergrowth from the forest. This practice allows new plants to sprout, which attracts animals such as wallabies.

▶ Aboriginals traditionally cook on open fires. Here, a woman cooks a type of bread, called damper, made from grass seeds.

52 Dense rainforests grow at the Equator, an imaginary line that encircles the Earth. The air is damp and hot, and it rains often. The trees teem with a wide variety of wildlife. Thick undergrowth makes it difficult to travel – and all too easy to get lost.

53 Rainforests hold many dangers. As well as large animals such as tigers, beware of poisonous snakes and huge spiders. Leeches stick to your skin and suck your blood, and mosquitoes and biting flies swarm around you. If you can light a fire in the damp conditions it will help to ward off insects.

▼ Although rarely deadly, bites from leeches, mosquitoes and spiders can be painful.

Cool, breathable clothing

Waterproof backpack

Sandals for wading across streams

Machete

Long trousers

Stout boots

▲ In the rainforest, it's best to keep well covered to avoid being bitten by insects.

RAINFOREST ANIMALS TO AVOID

Leeches feed on blood. They swell up, and drop off when they are full.

Some types of mosquitoes carry the deadly disease malaria.

The biggest tarantulas grow up to 30 centimetres across. Some are highly poisonous and hunt lizards and birds.

▲ Biting leafcutter ants will attack if disturbed. Tuck your trousers into your socks to stop them reaching your skin.

54

You could fall into a swamp in damp, waterlogged areas. Keep to clumps of grass and rushes, and test the ground ahead with a stick. If you find yourself sinking, try not to struggle. Lower yourself onto your knees, then lie back flat and try to swim or roll onto firm ground. Beware – swamps may be home to flesh-eating piranhas and crocodiles!

55

Rainforests contain all sorts of wild food. There are nuts and delicious fruits such as avocados, bananas and mangoes. However many plants are poisonous. A local guide or a survival handbook will show you the plants that are safe to eat.

▶ Hollow plants such as bamboo can be a source of safe drinking water.

Y.ıll

MALARIA

Symptoms:
Sweating
Violent shivering
Weakness
Vomiting

Action:
Take preventative drugs before you travel
Anti-malaria drugs are available if you can get to the nearest hospital

Menu   Contacts

56

In 1971, a German teenager was stranded alone in the Amazon Rainforest after a plane crash. Her father had once told her that heading downstream should lead to civilization. She followed this advice and reached a hunter's camp ten days later.

I DON'T BELIEVE IT!

In 2007 two men got lost on a hike in a rainforest in South America. They ran out of food, and lived on beetles and poisonous spiders. They had no idea they had camped just 4 kilometres from the nearest town!

Rainforest people

Amazon Rainforest

SOUTH AMERICA

▲ The Amazon Rainforest in South America is the world's largest rainforest.

57 Deep in the Amazon Rainforest live a people called the Yanomami. The rainforest provides them with food, as well as materials to build houses. They also use plant dyes to decorate their skin. The Amazon River provides water and a means of transport.

58 Yanomami people live in family groups, with each group in a circular hut called a *shabono*. Each family has a separate living space, which has hammocks slung from the rafters and a fire for cooking. Children play in the central area, which is also used for dancing and ceremonies.

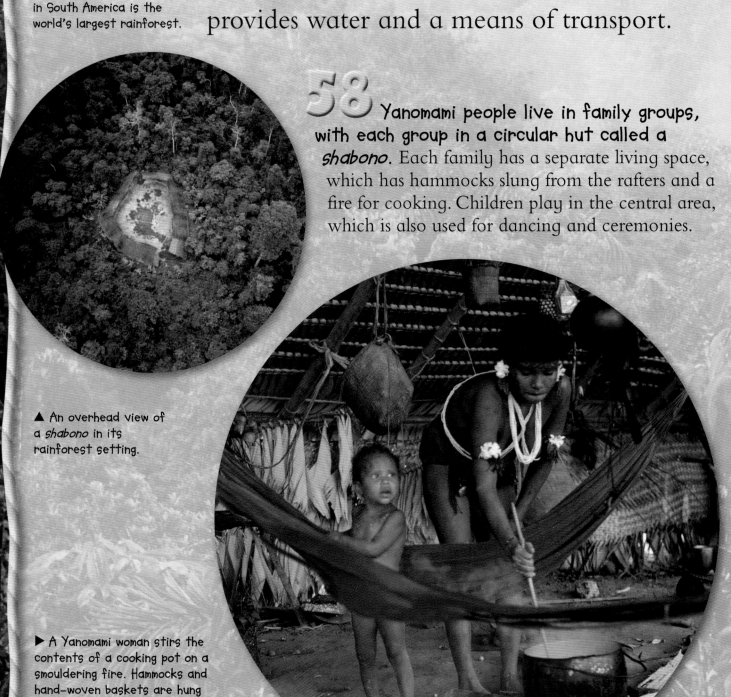

▲ An overhead view of a *shabono* in its rainforest setting.

▶ A Yanomami woman stirs the contents of a cooking pot on a smouldering fire. Hammocks and hand-woven baskets are hung from the ceiling.

59 **The Yanomami can identify hundreds of wild plants that can be eaten.** They create gardens by clearing small patches of forest to grow mainly crops such as cassava (a type of edible root), sweet potatoes and maize. Every few years the Yanomami clear new areas, and the old gardens return to the wild.

60 **Men hunt animals using blowpipes, and bows and arrows.** Some hunters coat their darts and arrows in deadly poison from the skin of brightly coloured poison-dart frogs. Others use a plant poison called curare.

61 **The Yanomami lived in the Amazon for thousands of years before Europeans arrived in the 1500s.** The newcomers brought diseases, and many native people died from them. Today, parts of the rainforest are at risk from logging, but some areas where the Yanomami live are now protected.

▶ As well as crops, the Yanomami grow fruits such as plantains and papayas, and cassava, which has to be cooked before it is eaten.

Plantains

Papaya

Cassava

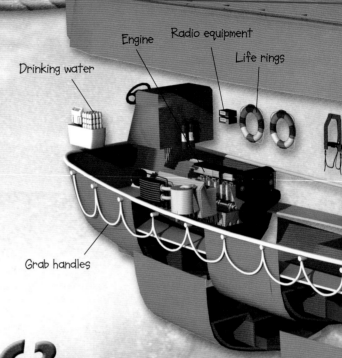

Drinking water

Engine

Radio equipment

Life rings

Grab handles

62 **The ocean is the most difficult environment to survive in and it covers nearly three-quarters of the Earth's surface.** Its dangers include violent storms, giant waves, and sea creatures such as sharks and killer whales.

DEADLIEST SHARKS

Tiger sharks grow to around 3 metres in length. Young sharks have dark stripes.
Danger: High risk of attack.

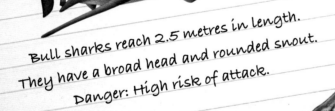

Bull sharks reach 2.5 metres in length. They have a broad head and rounded snout.
Danger: High risk of attack.

Great whites can grow to 4.5 metres in length. They have a white belly, grey back and a triangular-shaped dorsal fin.
Danger: Moderate risk of attack.

63 **In 1789, a mutiny on the HMS *Bounty* left Captain Bligh marooned in a small boat in the Pacific Ocean.** As the crew sailed away on the ship, Bligh and a few loyal men made for land in the little vessel. Using simple navigation equipment, Bligh crossed 6700 kilometres of ocean. After 47 days he reached land.

64 **Icebergs are a hazard in polar seas.** In 1912, the cruise liner *Titanic* hit an iceberg in the North Atlantic and sank quickly. Over 1500 of the 2223 people on board died because there were not enough lifeboats for everyone.

◀ Each year 10 to 20 people die from shark attacks. Tiger, bull and great white sharks are responsible for most of these.

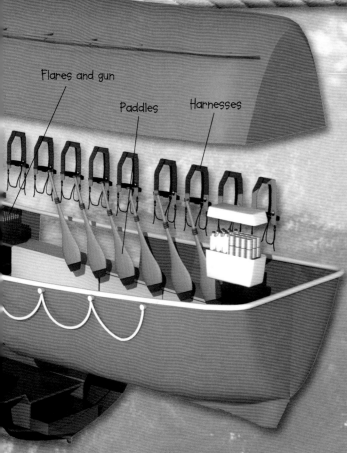

Flares and gun

Paddles

Harnesses

65 **If you have to abandon ship, grab a life jacket.** Put on warm clothing, including a hat and gloves – this will help you retain some body heat even in cold water. If you can, take chocolate or boiled sweets – they will give you energy. Try to enter cold water gradually, or the shock could kill you. If the ship is sinking, swim away to avoid being sucked down.

DEHYDRATION

Menu

Contacts

Symptoms:
Extreme thirst

Action:
Ration water – take small sips
Rest in the shade

▲ If a ship's lifeboat is launched it becomes a survival centre for those on board. It is stocked with essential supplies, such as food and water.

▼ Retain body warmth in cold water by crossing your arms and ankles, and keeping your head out of the water.

66 **Once in the water, inflate your life jacket or hold onto a floating object.** In cold water your body loses heat quickly, so try to keep your head dry. Don't exhaust yourself by trying to swim far. Instead, shout or blow a whistle to attract help.

MAKE A FLOATING AID

Make your trousers into a buoyancy aid.

1. Remove your trousers and knot the bottom of each leg tightly.
2. Holding the waist, swing the trousers over your head, so they fill with air.
3. Hold the waistband below the water to trap the air and hold the legs under your arms. You may need to blow in more air.

Adrift on a raft

67 In 1982, yachtsman Steve Callahan found himself in the middle of the ocean in a blow-up raft. Steve was taking part in a race across the Atlantic Ocean, in a boat he had built himself. On 15 January, he set sail from the Canary Islands, but his boat was damaged in a storm six days later, and began to sink.

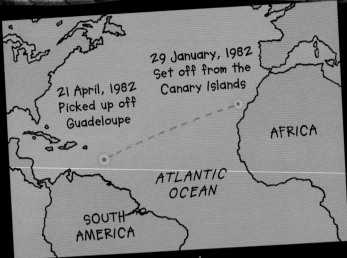

21 April, 1982 Picked up off Guadeloupe

29 January, 1982 Set off from the Canary Islands

AFRICA

ATLANTIC OCEAN

SOUTH AMERICA

▲ Steve's raft drifted 2900 kilometres west across the Atlantic Ocean. This shows his approximate route.

68 Steve had little time to abandon ship, but he kept calm. He was able to salvage some items from the sinking boat, including navigation charts, a torch, a knife, materials for collecting water and a survival manual. He also took food, a fishing kit and a pump for the raft.

▶ Steve took to his raft after his boat, *Napoleon Solo*, was wrecked by a storm during the night.

◀ Steve catches a dorado fish with his makeshift spear. He also used his spear to fend off sharks.

69 Steve was determined to stay alive. Out on the open water the midday sun was scorching, so he used his sleeping bag to keep covered up and cool. For food Steve used a homemade spear to catch fish, which he ate raw.

70 At sea, the biggest problem is the lack of fresh water. Steve was able to purify seawater using a solar still. This is a plastic dome filled with air. Seawater is fed into it and as the sun heats the air inside, the water evaporates. Fresh, non-salty water condenses on the sides of the dome and collects in a container.

▼ Steve was finally spotted by a fishing boat. He set a new record for solo survival on a blow-up raft – 76 days.

71 When Steve spotted a distant ship, he waved frantically. But nine ships passed by without seeing him. After 75 days at sea, he finally spotted a small island, and the next day a fishing boat rescued him. After reaching safety, he wrote a best-selling book about his ordeal.

72 If you are shipwrecked near an island, you may be able to swim to shore. Look out for razor-sharp reefs as you swim towards the beach. On the island, your first priority is to find fresh water.

Moisture from the leaves condenses and drips down

▶ Fresh water can be collected from leaves by tying a plastic bag over a branch.

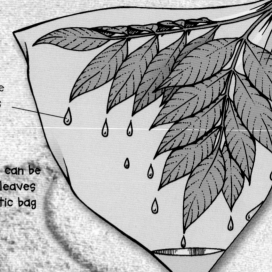

Use rope or vines to lash the branches together

Cover the frame with palm leaves

73 Build a temporary shelter on the beach. Look for useful items such as containers washed up on the shore. Surveying the island from a high point is a good idea. You may be able to spot an abandoned building, or even signs of human life.

▲ Build a sturdy A-frame shelter using branches and palm leaves.

Make a bamboo fishing spear

① Find a long piece of bamboo. Use your knife to split the end into four sections, 10 centimetres long.

② Cut the ends to make them pointed. Wrap twine or string in between the spikes to separate them.

③ Tie the ends of the twine together at the side. Your spear is ready to use to catch fish and crabs.

74 Coconuts are one of the main foods on tropical islands. The flesh can be eaten and the liquid inside is good to drink. There may also be fruit trees such as mangoes. Fish, shrimps and crabs lurk in rock pools, and may be caught by hand or using a spear.

◀ In the film *Cast Away* (2000), the sole survivor, Chuck Nolan, talks to a volleyball, which he has named 'Wilson'.

75 **People marooned on islands have to cope with loneliness.** Establishing a regular routine can help. In the film *Cast Away* (20th Century Fox / DreamWorks, 2000), a lone desert island survivor deals with loneliness by painting a face on a washed-up volleyball, and talking to it as if it were his friend.

76 **During World War II, lone Japanese soldiers were posted on islands in the Pacific Ocean.** Their task was to sabotage the enemy while staying hidden. Several soldiers remained on the islands long after the war was over. They survived by eating berries and beetles, and drinking rainwater. One officer finally surrendered 29 years after the end of the war.

Coconut

Crab

▲▶ Island foods include fruit, nuts, and shellfish such as crabs. You should only ever eat living shellfish.

Mango

Desert island survivor

77 In 1704, Scottish sailor Alexander Selkirk was marooned on the island of Juan Fernandez. Selkirk asked to be left on the island because he thought the ship he was serving on was unseaworthy. (It sank not long after!) But at the last minute, Selkirk changed his mind. He ran along the shore, shouting for the ship to come back, but it sailed away.

▲ The remote island of Juan Fernandez lies in the Pacific Ocean, off the coast of Chile.

78 At first, Selkirk camped in a cave on the beach. He ate shellfish that he found on the shore, but after several months, Selkirk was driven off the beach by sea lions. He went inland – a good move as there was more food: Turnips, cabbages and berries, and wild goats for meat and milk.

▶ Selkirk kept watch every day from the shore, hoping to spot a passing boat, until noisy sea lions forced him from his beach camp.

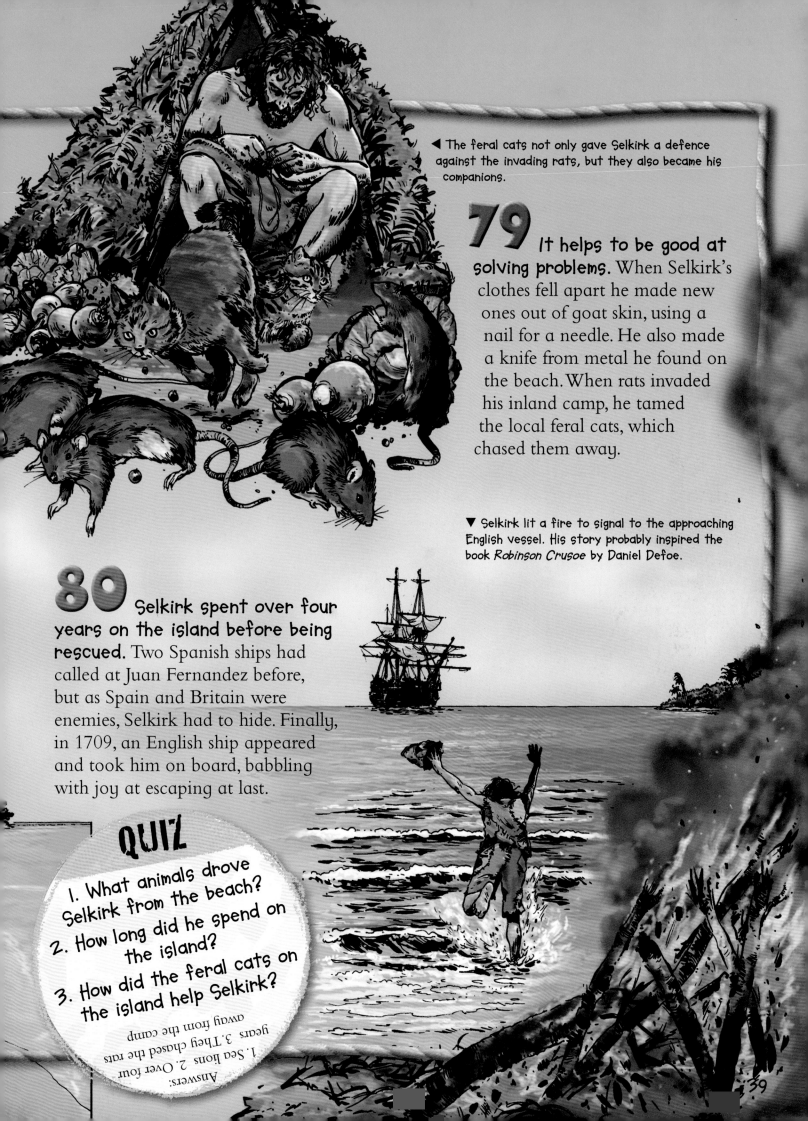

◀ The feral cats not only gave Selkirk a defence against the invading rats, but they also became his companions.

79

It helps to be good at solving problems. When Selkirk's clothes fell apart he made new ones out of goat skin, using a nail for a needle. He also made a knife from metal he found on the beach. When rats invaded his inland camp, he tamed the local feral cats, which chased them away.

▼ Selkirk lit a fire to signal to the approaching English vessel. His story probably inspired the book *Robinson Crusoe* by Daniel Defoe.

80

Selkirk spent over four years on the island before being rescued. Two Spanish ships had called at Juan Fernandez before, but as Spain and Britain were enemies, Selkirk had to hide. Finally, in 1709, an English ship appeared and took him on board, babbling with joy at escaping at last.

QUIZ

1. What animals drove Selkirk from the beach?
2. How long did he spend on the island?
3. How did the feral cats on the island help Selkirk?

Answers:
1. Sea lions 2. Over four years 3. They chased the rats away from the camp

NORTH AMERICAN PLATE

PACIFIC PLATE

81 Natural disasters, such as earthquakes, volcanic eruptions and tsunamis, plunge people into sudden and extreme danger. To survive, you have to be quick-thinking, determined – and sometimes very lucky.

◀▲ Taipei 101 in Taiwan is one of the world's tallest buildings. It is designed to withstand hurricanes and earthquakes. Inside is a huge pendulum ball, which moves to provide stability when the building sways.

82 Earthquakes are caused by the shifting of the rocky plates that form the Earth's crust. During a quake, the ground shakes, causing buildings to collapse. The ground can even split open.

WHAT TO DO IN AN EARTHQUAKE

1 Indoors, hide under a table or in a doorway.
2 Shield your head with your hands.
3 Outdoors, keep away from falling buildings.

83 When an earthquake strikes on the seabed, it can set off giant waves called tsunamis. They travel across the ocean at high speed. In open water they form low waves, but grow higher in shallow waters until they smash onto the shore.

WHAT TO DO IN A TSUNAMI

1 Get inland as fast as possible.
2 Head for the nearest high ground, such as a hill.
3 Do not return to low ground after the first wave – there may be more.

▶ Floating buoys relay signals from sensors on the seabed to give an early warning if a tsunami is likely.

RISTEK TSUNAMI

EURASIAN PLATE

INDO
AUSTRALIAN
PLATE

SOUTH
AMERICAN
PLATE

AFRICAN
PLATE

ANTARCTIC PLATE

KEY

▭ Plate boundary

▲ Volcano

▮ Earthquake zone

▮ Tsunami zone

◄ Areas at risk of volcanic eruptions, earthquakes and tsunamis often lie near the edges of the Earth's tectonic plates.

84 When a volcano erupts, red-hot lava and clouds of ash and gas spill down the slopes, and rocks fly through the air. Today, scientists are able to predict eruptions, so the surrounding areas can be evacuated in time. However, some eruptions occur without warning, over a short period of time.

85 In 1985, a volcano in the Andes Mountains erupted. Burning ash mixed with snow created a tide of mud that swept down into the Colombian town of Armero. Teenager Slaye Molina survived by racing uphill to a cemetery. She was rescued after three days, but many people died.

WHAT TO DO IN A VOLCANIC ERUPTION

1 Get out of the path of lava flows – you can usually outrun them.
2 Cover your nose and mouth with a damp cloth.
3 Head for high ground, but watch out for falling lava bombs.

▶ Sakurajima is an active volcano in Japan. Here, two men take cover in a lava bomb shelter during an eruption.

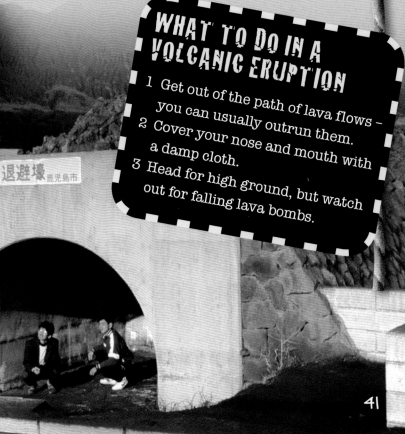

退避壕 鹿児島市

Wild weather

86 Extreme weather such as hurricanes, tornadoes and blizzards can be deadly. Hurricanes are huge spinning storms that form out at sea. Winds whirl at up to 300 kilometres an hour, causing flooding when they hit land.

87 Tornadoes are powerful columns of twisting air. Although they are much smaller than hurricanes, they can leave a trail of destruction. The funnel of air can suck up trees and cars. If a tornado is due, stay indoors, in a basement if possible. Outdoors, your car is not a safe place to stay. Lay flat in a ditch, or find a natural shelter such as a cave.

▶ A tornado weaves across South Dakota, USA. People called storm-chasers seek out these violent storms to witness the power of nature.

89 Flash floods can strike after violent thunderstorms. They are most dangerous in narrow river valleys where the water level rises quickly. The fast-moving torrent of water can sweep away trees and houses. If you are caught in a valley when sudden heavy rainfall occurs, make for high ground.

▲ In 2004 a flash flood wrecked the village of Boscastle in Cornwall, England, after a downpour.

88 When a hurricane hits, stay indoors and board up the windows. A basement is the safest place to shelter. If the hurricane is severe, people may be told to leave their homes. In the event of evacuation, make sure you have supplies of water, food, blankets and medicine – and above all, keep calm.

I DON'T BELIEVE IT!

US park ranger Roy Sullivan survived being struck by lightning seven times! In a thunderstorm, avoid lone trees, which can attract lightning. It's safer to stay in a car or lay on the ground.

▲ A bulldozer works to clear deep snow blocking a road. The chains on its tyres help its wheels grip in the snow.

90 Winter weather makes driving conditions treacherous. Blizzards are heavy snowstorms that can block roads. During severe hailstorms, balls of ice, sometimes as big as grapefruits, rain down and can smash car windscreens. In this case it may be safer to stop and shelter underneath the car.

91 Rainforests, deserts, oceans and other natural habitats are home to a host of dangerous animals. Big, powerful beasts such as bears harm fewer people than small, poisonous creatures, such as snakes and jellyfish. However, most dangerous of all is the mosquito, which carries the deadly disease malaria.

92 Elephants, hippos, lions and bears can charge without warning. The greatest risk of this is if you come between a mother and her young. If a hippo or elephant charges, run away, zigzagging from side to side. If a lion, bear or tiger approaches, you should face the animal while slowly backing away.

▼ Hippos are extremely dangerous animals, but an African fisherman has tamed this four-tonne female, called Africa, over the last 16 years.

QUIZ

1. What is the world's most dangerous animal?
2. What should you do if a lion approaches?
3. What creature was Bethany Hamilton bitten by?

Answers:
1. Mosquito 2. Face the animal and slowly back away 3. A tiger shark

Do not try this at home

93 Sharks are the scariest creatures in the oceans. In 2003, 13-year-old Bethany Hamilton was surfing in Hawaii when a tiger shark attacked her and bit off her arm. Luckily, she was with friends, who helped her back to shore to get help.

◄ After recovering, Bethany returned to surfing and has since won a major competition.

94 Snakes kill their prey by injecting it with venom or by squeezing it to death. In 2009, an African farmer was attacked by a 4-metre-long python, which wrapped itself around him. After a long struggle he managed to reach the mobile phone in his pocket to call for help.

▲ Steve Irwin learned to handle reptiles from a young age at his parents' zoo.

95 Australian wildlife expert Steve Irwin was known for his bravery in handling dangerous snakes and crocodiles. However in 2006, Steve was killed by a stingray when snorkelling at a coral reef. Although stingrays have poisonous spines, they rarely harm people.

ANIMALS DANGEROUS TO HUMANS
(Figures are estimates)

African lion	50+ deaths per year
Asian cobra	1000+ deaths per year
Box jellyfish	At least 64 recorded deaths since 1883
Cape buffalo	100+ deaths per year
Elephant	500+ deaths per year
Great white shark	Up to 10 attacks per year
Mosquito	2 million+ deaths per year
Saltwater crocodile	1–2 deaths per year in Australia, probably more worldwide

Box jellyfish

Elephant

Saltwater crocodile

Getting to safety

96 In an emergency, you must decide whether to stay put and wait for rescue, or try to reach safety yourself. If you have enough food, water and warm clothing, it's generally best to stay where you are.

97 If no one knows you are in danger, you need to signal for help. SOS ('Save Our Souls') is a distress signal that is understood all over the world. 'SOS' in large letters on the ground may be seen by low-flying planes. You could also send an SOS in Morse code using a whistle (three short blasts, three long blasts, three short blasts).

98 The easiest way to get help is by using a mobile phone. But in remote places it may not work. Alternatively, a flare can send a long-distance distress sign that is visible from land or air.

▼ A signal flare lets off a plume of brightly coloured smoke that can be seen for many kilometres.

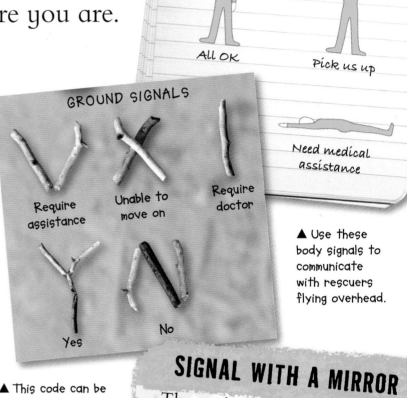

BODY SIGNALS

Land here (point in direction)

Need mechanical help

All OK

Pick us up

Need medical assistance

▲ Use these body signals to communicate with rescuers flying overhead.

GROUND SIGNALS

Require assistance

Unable to move on

Require doctor

Yes

No

▲ This code can be used to signal to planes. Lay branches on clear ground and make the signs as big as you can.

SIGNAL WITH A MIRROR

The sun's reflection on a mirror can be seen from a great distance.

You will need:
small mirror   friend

1. Go to a local park or playing field. Stand a good distance away from your friend.
2. Hold the mirror up so it catches the light. Hold your other arm out and part your fingers so you can see your friend through the gap.
3. Angle the mirror so the reflection hits your parted fingers and aims at your target.
Did your friend see the reflections?

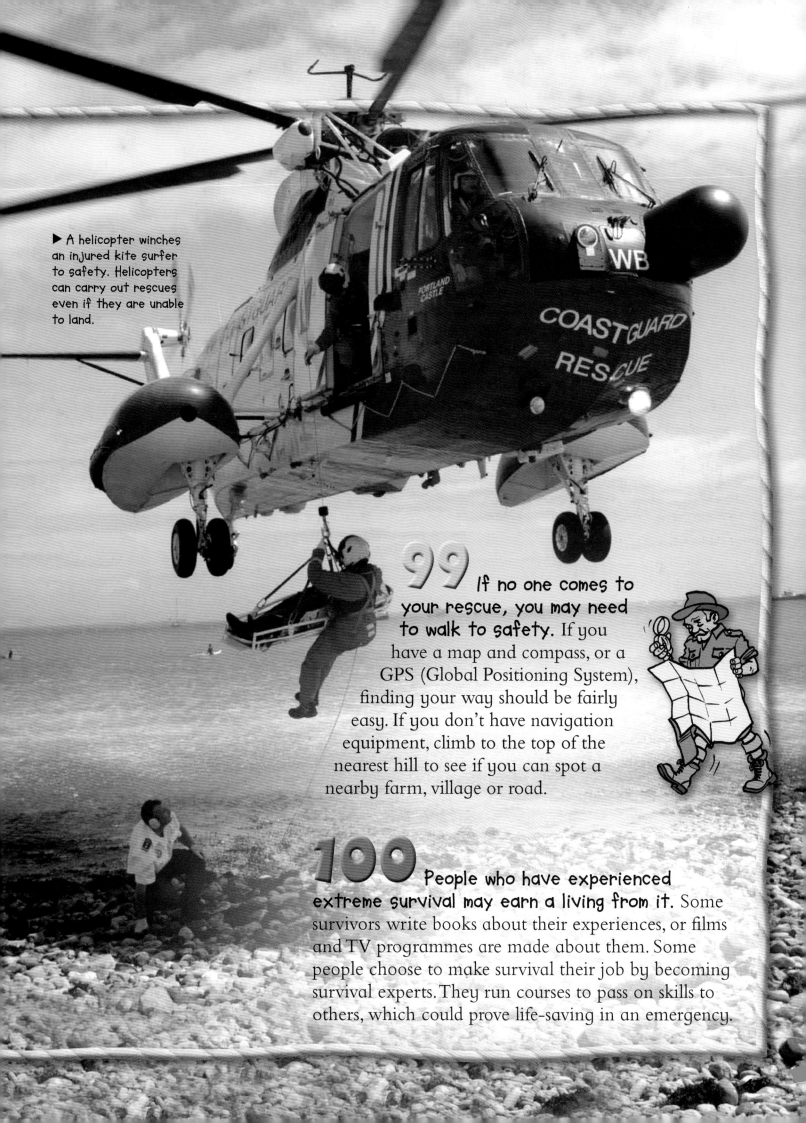

▶ A helicopter winches an injured kite surfer to safety. Helicopters can carry out rescues even if they are unable to land.

99 If no one comes to your rescue, you may need to walk to safety. If you have a map and compass, or a GPS (Global Positioning System), finding your way should be fairly easy. If you don't have navigation equipment, climb to the top of the nearest hill to see if you can spot a nearby farm, village or road.

100 People who have experienced extreme survival may earn a living from it. Some survivors write books about their experiences, or films and TV programmes are made about them. Some people choose to make survival their job by becoming survival experts. They run courses to pass on skills to others, which could prove life-saving in an emergency.

Index

Entries in **bold** refer to main subject entries. Entries in *italics* refer to illustrations.